THE
TRIUMPH
OF
ACHILLES

LOUISE GLÜCK

THE TRIUMPH OF ACHILLES

THE ECCO PRESS
NEW YORK

PS
3557
L8
T7
1985

ACKNOWLEDGMENTS

ANTAEUS: Horse
THE NEW REPUBLIC: A Parable
Liberation
THE NEW YORKER: Brooding Likeness
Night Song
PEQUOD: The Triumph of Achilles
The Reproach
Adult Grief
YALE REVIEW: Mock Orange
SALMAGUNDI: First Goodbye

*To Samn Stockwell, John Dranow and Ellen Bryant Voigt,
my deepest gratitude.*

First published by The Ecco Press in 1985
18 West 30th Street, New York, N.Y. 10001
Printed in the United States of America
Designed by JoAnne Metsch

Library of Congress Cataloging in Publication Data

Glück, Louise, 1943–
The triumph of Achilles.

I. Title.
PS3557.L8T7 1985   811'.54   85-10249
ISBN 0-88001-081-9

Publication of this book was made possible
in part by a grant from The National Endowment
for the Arts.

FIRST EDITION

TO CHARLES CLAY DAHLBERG

First blossom in the wet grass—
O my body, you were given
only the one task, why
will you not repeat it?

"But if, as some say . . . his suffering was only an appearance,
then why am I a prisoner, and why do I long to fight with the
wild beasts?"   —Ignatius

"Joey was beginning to know good from evil. And whoever
does that is committed to live a human existence on earth."
                                    —Bruno Bettelheim

CONTENTS

ONE

MOCK ORANGE

It is not the moon, I tell you.
It is these flowers
lighting the yard.

I hate them.
I hate them as I hate sex,
the man's mouth
sealing my mouth, the man's
paralyzing body—

and the cry that always escapes,
the low, humiliating
premise of union—

In my mind tonight
I hear the question and pursuing answer
fused in one sound
that mounts and mounts and then
is split into the old selves,
the tired antagonisms. Do you see?
We were made fools of.
And the scent of mock orange
drifts through the window.

How can I rest?
How can I be content
when there is still
that odor in the world?

METAMORPHOSIS

1. Night

The angel of death flies
low over my father's bed.
Only my mother sees. She and my father
are alone in the room.

She bends over him to touch
his hand, his forehead. She is
so used to mothering
that now she strokes his body
as she would the other children's,
first gently, then
inured to suffering.

Nothing is any different.
Even the spot on the lung
was always there.

2. Metamorphosis

My father has forgotten me
in the excitement of dying.
Like a child who will not eat,
he takes no notice of anything.

I sit at the edge of his bed
while the living circle us
like so many tree stumps.

Once, for the smallest
fraction of an instant, I thought
he was alive in the present again;
then he looked at me
as a blind man stares
straight into the sun, since
whatever it could do to him
is done already.

Then his flushed face
turned away from the contract.

3. For My Father

I'm going to live without you
as I learned once
to live without my mother.
You think I don't remember that?
I've spent my whole life trying to remember.

Now, after so much solitude,
death doesn't frighten me,
not yours, not mine either.
And those words, *the last time*,
have no power over me. I know
intense love always leads to mourning.

For once, your body doesn't frighten me.
From time to time, I run my hand over your face
lightly, like a dustcloth.
What can shock me now? I feel
no coldness that can't be explained.
Against your cheek, my hand is warm
and full of tenderness.

BROODING LIKENESS

I was born in the month of the bull,
the month of heaviness,
or of the lowered, the destructive head,
or of purposeful blindness. So I know, beyond the shadowed
patch of grass, the stubborn one, the one who doesn't look up,
still senses the rejected world. It is
a stadium, a well of dust. And you who watch him
looking down in the face of death, what do you know
of commitment? If the bull lives
one controlled act of revenge, be satisfied
that in the sky, like you, he is always moving,
not of his own accord but through the black field
like grit caught on a wheel, like shining freight.

EXILE

He did not pretend
to be one of them. They did not require
a poet, a spokesman. He saw
the dog's heart, the working
lips of the parasite—
He himself preferred
to listen in the small apartments
as a man would check his camera at the museum,
to express his commitment through silence:
there is no other exile.
The rest is egotism; in the bloody street,
the I, the impostor—
He *was* there, obsessed with revolution,
in his own city,
daily climbing the wooden stairs
that were not a path
but necessary repetitions
and for twenty years
making no poetry
of what he saw: nor did he forfeit
great achievement. In his mind,
there could be no outcry that did not equate
his choice with their imprisonment
and he would not allow
the gift to be tainted.

WINTER MORNING

1.

Today, when I woke up, I asked myself
why did Christ die? Who knows
the meaning of such questions?

It was a winter morning, unbelievably cold.
So the thoughts went on,
from each question came
another question, like a twig from a branch,
like a branch from a black trunk.

2.

At a time like this
a young woman traveled through the desert settlements
looking neither forward nor backward,
sitting in perfect composure on the tired animal
as the child stirred, still sealed in its profound attachment—
The husband walked slightly ahead, older, out of place;
increasingly, the mule stumbled, the path becoming
difficult in darkness, though they persisted
in a world like our world, not ruled
by man but by a statue in heaven—

3.

Above the crowds representing
humankind, the lost
citizens of a remote time,

the insulted body
raised on a cross like a criminal
to die publicly
above Jerusalem, the shimmering city

while in great flocks
birds circled the body, not partial
to this form over the others

since men were all alike,
defeated by the air,

whereas in air
the body of a bird becomes a banner:

But the lesson that was needed
was another lesson.

4.
In untrustworthy springtime
he was seen moving
among us like one of us

in green Judea, covered with the veil of life,
among the olive trees, among the many shapes
blurred by spring,

stopping to eat and rest, in obvious need,
among the thousand flowers,
some planted, some distributed by wind,

like all men, seeking
recognition on earth,
so that he spoke to the disciples

in a man's voice, lifting his intact hand:
was it the wind that spoke?
Or stroked Mary's hair, until she raised her eyes

no longer wounded
by his coldness, by his needless destruction
of the flesh which was her fulfillment—

This was not the sun.
This was Christ in his cocoon of light:

so they swore. And there were other witnesses
though they were all blind,
they were all swayed by love—

5.
Winters are long here.
The road a dark gray, the maples gray, silvered with lichen,
and the sun low on the horizon,
white on blue; at sunset, vivid orange-red.

When I shut my eyes, it vanishes.
When I open my eyes, it reappears.
Outside, spring rain, a pulse, a film on the window.

And suddenly it is summer, all puzzling fruit and light.

SEATED FIGURE

It was as though you were a man in a wheelchair,
your legs cut off at the knee.
But I wanted you to walk.
I wanted us to walk like lovers,
arm in arm in the summer evening,
and believed so powerfully in that projection
that I had to speak, I had to press you to stand.
Why did you let me speak?
I took your silence as I took the anguish in your face,
as part of the effort to move—
It seemed I stood forever, holding out my hand.
And all that time, you could no more heal yourself
than I could accept what I saw.

MYTHIC FRAGMENT

When the stern god
approached me with his gift
my fear enchanted him
so that he ran more quickly
through the wet grass, as he insisted,
to praise me. I saw captivity
in praise; against the lyre,
I begged my father in the sea
to save me. When
the god arrived, I was nowhere,
I was in a tree forever. Reader,
pity Apollo: at the water's edge,
I turned from him, I summoned
my invisible father—as
I stiffened in the god's arms,
of his encompassing love
my father made
no other sign from the water.

HYACINTH

1.
Is that an attitude for a flower, to stand
like a club at the walk; poor slain boy,
is that a way to show
gratitude to the gods? White
with colored hearts, the tall flowers
sway around you, all the other boys,
in the cold spring, as the violets open.

2.
There were no flowers in antiquity
but boys' bodies, pale, perfectly imagined.
So the gods sank to human shape with longing.
In the field, in the willow grove,
Apollo sent the courtiers away.

3.
And from the blood of the wound
a flower sprang, lilylike, more brilliant
than the purples of Tyre.
Then the god wept: his vital grief
flooded the earth.

4.
Beauty dies: that is the source
of creation. Outside the ring of trees
the courtiers could hear
the dove's call transmit
its uniform, its inborn sorrow—
They stood listening, among the rustling willows.
Was this the god's lament?

They listened carefully. And for a short time
all sound was sad.

5.
There is no other immortality:
in the cold spring, the purple violets open.
And yet, the heart is black,
there is its violence frankly exposed.
Or is it not the heart at the center
but some other word?
And now someone is bending over them,
meaning to gather them—

6.
They could not wait
in exile forever.
Through the glittering grove
the courtiers ran
calling the name
of their companion
over the birds' noise,
over the willows' aimless sadness.
Well into the night they wept,
their clear tears
altering no earthly color.

THE TRIUMPH OF ACHILLES

In the story of Patroclus
no one survives, not even Achilles
who was nearly a god.
Patroclus resembled him; they wore
the same armor.

Always in these friendships
one serves the other, one is less than the other:
the hierarchy
is always apparent, though the legends
cannot be trusted—
their source is the survivor,
the one who has been abandoned.

What were the Greek ships on fire
compared to this loss?

In his tent, Achilles
grieved with his whole being
and the gods saw

he was a man already dead, a victim
of the part that loved,
the part that was mortal.

BASKETS

1.
It is a good thing,
in the marketplace
the old woman trying to decide
among the lettuces,
impartial, weighing the heads,
examining
the outer leaves, even
sniffing them to catch
a scent of earth
of which, on one head,
some trace remains—not
the substance but
the residue—so
she prefers it to
the other, more
estranged heads, it
being freshest: nodding
briskly at the vendor's wife,
she makes this preference known,
an old woman, yet
vigorous in judgment.

2.
The circle of the world—
in its midst, a dog
sits at the edge of the fountain.
The children playing there,
coming and going from the village,
pause to greet him, the impulsive
losing interest in play,
in the little village of sticks

adorned with blue fragments of pottery;
they squat beside the dog
who stretches in the hot dust:
arrows of sunlight
dance around him.
Now, in the field beyond,
some great event is ending.
In twos and threes, boldly
swinging their shirts,
the athletes stroll away, scattering
red and blue, blue and dazzling purple
over the plain ground,
over the trivial surface.

3.
Lord, who gave me
my solitude, I watch
the sun descending:
in the marketplace
the stalls empty, the remaining children
bicker at the fountain—
But even at night, when it can't be seen,
the flame of the sun
still heats the pavements.
That's why, on earth,
so much life's sprung up,
because the sun maintains
steady warmth at its periphery.
Does this suggest your meaning:
that the game resumes,
in the dust beneath
the infant god of the fountain;
there is nothing fixed,
there is no assurance of death—

4.
I take my basket to the brazen market,
to the gathering place.
I ask you, how much beauty
can a person bear? It is
heavier than ugliness, even the burden
of emptiness is nothing beside it.
Crates of eggs, papaya, sacks of yellow lemons—
I am not a strong woman. It isn't easy
to want so much, to walk
with such a heavy basket, either
bent reed, or willow.

LIBERATION

My mind is clouded,
I cannot hunt anymore.
I lay my gun over the tracks of the rabbit.

It was as though I became that creature
who could not decide
whether to flee or be still
and so was trapped in the pursuer's eyes—

And for the first time I knew
those eyes have to be blank
because it is impossible
to kill and question at the same time.

Then the shutter snapped,
the rabbit went free. He flew
through the empty forest

that part of me
that was the victim.
Only victims have a destiny.

And the hunter, who believed
whatever struggles
begs to be torn apart:

that part is paralyzed.

TWO

THE EMBRACE

She taught him the gods. Was it teaching? He went on
hating them, but in the long evenings of obsessive talk,
as he listened, they became real. Not that they changed.
They never came to seem innately human.
In the firelight, he watched her face.
But she would not be touched; she had rejected
the original need. Then in the darkness he would lead her
    back—
above the trees, the city rose in a kind of splendor
as all that is wild comes to the surface.

MARATHON

1. Last Letter

Weeping, standing still—then going out again into the garden.
In the field, white heads of dandelions making rows of saints,
now bending, now stiff with awe—
and at the edge, a hare: his eyes fixed, terrified.
Silence. Herds of bells—

Without thinking, I knelt in the grass, like someone meaning
    to pray.
When I tried to stand again, I couldn't move,
my legs were utterly rigid. Does grief change you like that?
Through the birches, I could see the pond.
The sun was cutting small white holes in the water.

I got up finally; I walked down to the pond.
I stood there, brushing the grass from my skirt, watching myself,
like a girl after her first lover
turning slowly at the bathroom mirror, naked, looking for a sign.
But nakedness in women is always a pose.
I was not transfigured. I would never be free.

2. Song of the River

Once we were happy, we had no memories.
For all the repetition, nothing happened twice.
We were always walking parallel to a river
with no sense of progression
though the trees across from us
were sometimes birch, sometimes cypress—
the sky was blue, a matrix of blue glass.

While, in the river, things were going by—
a few leaves, a child's boat painted red and white,
its sail stained by the water—

As they passed, on the surface we could see ourselves;
we seemed to drift
apart and together, as the river
linked us forever, though up ahead
were other couples, choosing souvenirs.

3. The Encounter

You came to the side of the bed
and sat staring at me.
Then you kissed me—I felt
hot wax on my forehead.
I wanted it to leave a mark:
that's how I knew I loved you.
Because I wanted to be burned, stamped,
to have something in the end—
I drew the gown over my head;
a red flush covered my face and shoulders.
It will run its course, the course of fire,
setting a cold coin on the forehead, between the eyes.
You lay beside me; your hand moved over my face
as though you had felt it also—
you must have known, then, how I wanted you.
We will always know that, you and I.
The proof will be my body.

4. Song of Obstacles

When my lover touches me, what I feel in my body
is like the first movement of a glacier over the earth,
as the ice shifts, dislodging great boulders, hills
of solemn rock: so, in the forests, the uprooted trees
become a sea of disconnected limbs—
And, where there are cities, these dissolve too,
the sighing gardens, all the young girls
eating chocolates in the courtyard, slowly
scattering the colored foil: then, where the city was,
the ore, the unearthed mysteries: so I see
that ice is more powerful than rock, than mere resistance—

Then for us, in its path, time doesn't pass,
not even an hour.

5. Night Song

Look up into the light of the lantern.
Don't you see? The calm of darkness
is the horror of Heaven.

We've been apart too long, too painfully separated.
How can you bear to dream,
to give up watching? I think you must be dreaming,
your face is full of mild expectancy.

I need to wake you, to remind you that there isn't a future.
That's why we're free. And now some weakness in me
has been cured forever, so I'm not compelled
to close my eyes, to go back, to rectify—

The beach is still; the sea, cleansed of its superfluous life,
opaque, rocklike. In mounds, in vegetal clusters,
seabirds sleep on the jetty. Terns, assassins—

You're tired; I can see that.
We're both tired, we have acted a great drama.
Even our hands are cold, that were like kindling.
Our clothes are scattered on the sand; strangely enough,
they never turned to ashes.

I have to tell you what I've learned, that I know now
what happens to the dreamers.
They don't feel it when they change. One day
they wake, they dress, they are old.

Tonight I'm not afraid
to feel the revolutions. How can you want sleep
when passion gives you that peace?
You're like me tonight, one of the lucky ones.
You'll get what you want. You'll get your oblivion.

6. The Beginning

I had come to a strange city, without belongings:
in the dream, it was your city, I was looking for you.
Then I was lost, on a dark street lined with fruit stands.

There was only one fruit: blood oranges.
The markets made displays of them, beautiful displays—
how else could they compete? And each arrangement had, at
    its center,
one fruit, cut open.

Then I was on a boulevard, in brilliant sunlight.
I was running; it was easy to run, since I had nothing.
In the distance, I could see your house; a woman knelt in the
    yard.
There were roses everywhere; in waves, they climbed the high
    trellis.

Then what began as love for you
became a hunger for structure: I could hear
the woman call to me in common kindness, knowing
I wouldn't ask for you anymore—

So it was settled: I could have a childhood there.
Which came to mean being always alone.

7. First Goodbye

You can join the others now,
body that wouldn't let my body rest,
go back to the world, to avenues, the ordered
depths of the parks, like great terminals
that never darken: a stranger's waiting for you
in a hundred rooms. Go back to them,
to increment and limitation: near the centered rose,
you watch her peel an orange
so the dyed rind falls in petals on her plate. This
is mastery, whose active
mode is dissection: the enforced light
shines on the blade. Sooner or later
you'll begin to dream of me. I don't envy you
those dreams. I can imagine how my face looks,
burning like that, afflicted with desire—lowered
face of your invention—how the mouth betrays
the isolated greed of the lover
as it magnifies and then destroys:
I don't envy you that visitation.
And the women lying there—who wouldn't pity them,
the way they turn to you, the way
they struggle to be visible. They make
a place for you in bed, a white excavation.
Then the sacrament: your bodies pieced together,
churning, churning, till the heat leaves them entirely—

Sooner or later you will call my name,
cry of loss, mistaken
cry of recognition, of arrested need
for someone who exists in memory: no voice
carries to that kingdom.

8. Song of Invisible Boundaries

Last night I dreamed we were in Venice;
today, we are in Venice. Now, lying here,
I think there are no boundaries to my dreams,
nothing we won't share.
So there is nothing to describe. We're interchangeable
with anyone, in joy
changed to a mute couple.

Then why did we worship clarity,
to speak, in the end, only each other's names,
to speak, as now, not even whole words,
only vowels?

Finally, this is what we craved,
this lying in the bright light without distinction—
we who would leave behind
exact records.

9. Marathon

I was not meant to hear
the two of them talking.
But I could feel the light of the torch
stop trembling, as though it had been
set on a table. I was not to hear
the one say to the other
how best to arouse me,
with what words, what gestures,
nor to hear the description of my body,
how it responded, what
it would not do. My back was turned.
I studied the voices, soon distinguishing
the first, which was deeper, closer,
from that of the replacement.
For all I know, this happens
every night: somebody waking me, then
the first teaching the second.
What happens afterward
occurs far from the world, at a depth
where only the dream matters
and the bond with any one soul
is meaningless; you throw it away.

SUMMER

Remember the days of our first happiness,
how strong we were, how dazed by passion,
lying all day, then all night in the narrow bed,
sleeping there, eating there too: it was summer,
it seemed everything had ripened
at once. And so hot we lay completely uncovered.
Sometimes the wind rose; a willow brushed the window.

But we were lost in a way, didn't you feel that?
The bed was like a raft; I felt us drifting
far from our natures, toward a place where we'd discover
    nothing.
First the sun, then the moon, in fragments,
shone through the willow.
Things anyone could see.

Then the circles closed. Slowly the nights grew cool;
the pendant leaves of the willow
yellowed and fell. And in each of us began
a deep isolation, though we never spoke of this,
of the absence of regret.
We were artists again, my husband.
We could resume the journey.

THREE

THE REPROACH

You have betrayed me, Eros.
You have sent me
my true love.

On a high hill you made
his clear gaze;
my heart was not
so hard as your arrow.

What is a poet
without dreams?
I lie awake; I feel
actual flesh upon me,
meaning to silence me—
Outside, in the blackness
over the olive trees,
a few stars.

I think this is a bitter insult:
that I prefer to walk
the coiled paths of the garden,
to walk beside the river
glittering with drops
of mercury. I like to lie
in the wet grass beside the river,
running away, Eros,
not openly, with other men,
but discreetly, coldly—

All my life
I have worshiped the wrong gods.
When I watch the trees
on the other side,
the arrow in my heart
is like one of them,
swaying and quivering.

THE END OF THE WORLD

1. Terra Nova

A place without associations—
Where, in the other country, there were mountains
so the mind was made to discover
words for containment, and so on,
here there was water, an extension of the brilliant city.
As for detail: where there had been, before,
nurturing slopes of grass on which, at evening or before rain,
the Charolais would lie, their many eyes
affixed to the traveler, here
there was clay. And yet it blossomed astoundingly:
beside the house, camellia, periwinkle, rosemary in crushing
    profusion—
in his heart, he was a lover again,
calling *now, now,* not restricted
to *once* or *in the old days.* He lay on his back in the wild fennel.
But in fact he was an old man.
Sixty years ago, he took his mother's hand. It was May, his
    birthday.
They were walking in the orchard, in the continuous present,
gathering apple blossoms. Then she wanted him to watch the
    sun;
they had to stand together as it sank in the possessive earth.
How short it seemed, that lifetime of waiting—
this red star blazing over the bay
was all the light of his childhood
that had followed him here.

2. The Tribute

In that period of strange calm
he wandered down stone steps to the wide harbor:
he was moved; the lights of the city moved him deeply
and it seemed the earth was being offered to him
as a source of awe—he had no wish to change.
He had written, he had built his temple.
So he justified a need to sacrifice.
He leaned against the railing: in the dark bay, he saw the city
    waver;
cells of light floated on the water, they rocked gently, held by
    white threads.
Behind him, on the steps, he heard a man and woman
arguing with great intensity.
In a poem, he could bring them together
like two pieces of a broken toy that could be joined again—
Then the voices ceased, replaced by sighs, rustlings, the little
    sounds
of which he had no knowledge
though the wind persisted
in conveying them to where he stood,
and with them all the odors of summer.

3. The End of the World

It is difficult to describe, coming as it still does
to each person at a different time.
Unique, terrible—and in the sky, uncanny brilliance
substituting for the humanizing sun.
So the blessed kneel, the lucky who expect nothing,
while those who loved the world
are returned by suffering
to what precedes attachment, namely
hatred of pain. Now the bitter are confirmed
in loneliness: they watch the winter sun
mockingly lower itself over the bare earth,
making nothing live—in this light
god approaches the dying.
Not the true god, of course. There is no god
who will save one man.

THE MOUNTAIN

My students look at me expectantly.
I explain to them that the life of art is a life
of endless labor. Their expressions
hardly change; they need to know
a little more about endless labor.
So I tell them the story of Sisyphus,
how he was doomed to push
a rock up a mountain, knowing nothing
would come of this effort
but that he would repeat it
indefinitely. I tell them
there is joy in this, in the artist's life,
that one eludes
judgment, and as I speak
I am secretly pushing a rock myself,
slyly pushing it up the steep
face of a mountain. Why do I lie
to these children? They aren't listening,
they aren't deceived, their fingers
tapping at the wooden desks—
So I retract
the myth; I tell them it occurs
in hell, and that the artist lies
because he is obsessed with attainment,
that he perceives the summit
as that place where he will live forever,
a place about to be
transformed by his burden: with every breath,
I am standing at the top of the mountain.
Both my hands are free. And the rock has added
height to the mountain.

A PARABLE

It was an epoch of heroes.
So this young boy, this nobody,
making his way from one plain to another,
picks up a small stone among the cold, unspecified
rocks of the hillside. It is a pleasant day.
At his feet, normal vegetation, the few white flowers
like stars, the leaves woolly, sage-green:
at the bottom of the hill are corpses.

Who is the enemy? Who has distributed
the compact bodies of the Jews
in this unprecedented silence? Disguised in dirt,
the scattered army sees the beast, Goliath,
towering above the childish shepherd.
They shut their eyes. And all the level earth
becomes the shattered surface of a sea, so disruptive
is that fall. In the ensuing dust, David
lifts his hand: then it is his, the hushed,
completed kingdom—

Fellow Jews, to plot a hero's journey
is to trace a mountain: hero to god, god to ruler.
At the precipice, the moment we don't want to hear about—
the stone is gone; now
the hand is the weapon.

On the palace roof, King David stares across
the shining city of Jerusalem
into the face of Bathsheba and perceives
his own amplified desire. At heart, he feels nothing.
She is like a flower in a tub of water. Above his head,
the clouds move. And it comes to him he has attained
all he is capable of dreaming.

DAY WITHOUT NIGHT

The angel of god pushed the child's hand
away from the jewels, toward the burning coal.

1.
The image
of truth is fire: it mounts
the fortress of heaven.

Have you never felt
its obvious power?
Even a child
is capable of this joy.

Apparently,
a like sun
burns in hell. It *is* hell,
day without night.

2.
It was as though Pharaoh's daughter
had brought home a lion cub
and for a few weeks
passed it off as a cat.
You did not press this woman.
She said she came upon
a child in the rushes;
each time she told the story,
her handmaidens recreated
their interminable chorus of sighs.
It had to be:
A little prince. A little lion cub.

3.
And then with almost no encouragement
a sign came: for awhile
the child is like
a grandson to Pharaoh.
Then he squirms; on Pharaoh's lap
he reaches for the crown of Egypt—

4.
So Pharaoh set before the child
two trays, one of rubies, one of burning embers:

Light of my heart, the world
is set before you:
fire on either side, fire
without alternative—

5.
It was like a magic act: all you saw
was the child move; the same hand that took
such active interest in
the wealth of Egypt showed
this sudden preference for a pile of coal.
You never saw the actual angel.
And to complete the act,
the child maimed himself—
And a cry arose,
almost as though a person
were in hell,
where there is nothing to do
but see—

6.
Moses
lay in the rushes:
he could see

only in one direction,
his perspective being
narrowed by the basket.
What he saw
was great light, like
a wing hovering.
And god said to him,
"You can be the favored one,
the one who tastes fire
and cannot speak,
or you can die now
and let the others
stay in Egypt: tell them
it was better to die in Egypt,
better to litter the river
with your corpse, than face
a new world."

7.
It was as though a soul emerged,
independent of the angel,
a conscious being choosing
not to enter paradise—
at the same time, the true
sun was setting.
As it touched the water
by necessity the mirrored sun rose
to meet it from
the depths of the river:
Then the cry ended.
Or was hidden
in the stammering
of the redeemer—

8.
The context
of truth is darkness: it sweeps
the deserts of Israel.

Are you taken in
by lights, by illusions?

Here is your path to god,
who has no name, whose hand
is invisible: a trick
of moonlight on the dark water.

ELMS

All day I tried to distinguish
need from desire. Now, in the dark,
I feel only bitter sadness for us,
the builders, the planers of wood,
because I have been looking
steadily at these elms
and seen the process that creates
the writhing, stationary tree
is torment, and have understood
it will make no forms but twisted forms.

ADULT GRIEF

Because you were foolish enough to love one place,
now you are homeless, an orphan
in a succession of shelters.
You did not prepare yourself sufficiently.
Before your eyes, two people were becoming old;
I could have told you two deaths were coming.
There has never been a parent
kept alive by a child's love.

Now, of course, it's too late—
you were trapped in the romance of fidelity.
You kept going back, clinging
to two people you hardly recognized
after what they'd endured.

If once you could have saved yourself,
now that time's past: you were obstinate, pathetically
blind to change. Now you have nothing:
for you, home is a cemetery.
I've seen you press your face against the granite markers—
you are the lichen, trying to grow there.
But you will not grow,
you will not let yourself
obliterate anything.

for E. V.

HAWK'S SHADOW

Embracing in the road
for some reason I no longer remember
and then drawing apart, seeing
that shape ahead—how close was it?
We looked up to where the hawk
hovered with its kill; I watched them
veering toward West Hill, casting
their one shadow in the dirt, the all-inclusive
shape of the predator—
Then they disappeared. And I thought:
one shadow. Like the one we made,
you holding me.

FROM THE JAPANESE

1.
A cat stirs in the material world.
And suddenly sunlight pours into the room
as though somewhere a blind had been opened.
And on the floor, the white bars of a ladder appear.

2.
Gwen is sobbing in the front yard; she is three.
The Spanish maid strokes her hair—Gwen
is bilingual; she dries her eyes,
a few petals falling from the jacaranda tree.

Now the door opens: here is Jack, the athlete, in his combat
  boots.
For the next hour he runs
first away from, then toward his family.

And here is Trixie, roaming the driveway,
huge in comparison
to the rigid bird. Boring bird,
that will not chirp and fight anymore.
She flicks it once or twice,
under the grapefruit, under the lemon tree.

Early summer: fog covers the mountains.
Under each tree, a doily of shade.

3.
At first, I saw you everywhere.
Now only in certain things,
at longer intervals.

4.
We were walking in the Japanese gardens
among the bare cherry trees,
a path you chose
deliberately in desolate November

as though I myself had ordered down
the petals, the black
nuggets of the fruit—

Nearby, a boy sailed his wooden boat,
home and away, home and away.
Then the thread snapped; the boat
was carried toward the waterfall.

"From this moment I will never know
ease," you said, "since you have lied to me,
nor joy." The boy
covered his face with his hands.

There is another world,
neither air nor water
but an emptiness which now
a symbol has entered.

5.
The cat
misses her master.
She climbs the brick wall,

a feat
Gwen determines
to copy: loud
objections from the Spanish maid.

Tears, shuffling. At the water's edge,
the boy finally
lowered his hands.
He had a new toy, a thread
tied to a lost thing—

Twilight: in her blue sombrero,
Gwen reconstructs the summer garden.

6.
Alone, watching the moon rise:
tonight, a full circle,
like a woman's eye passing over abundance.

This is the most it will ever be.
Above the blank street, the imperfections
solved by night—

Like our hearts: darkness
showed us their capacity.
Our full hearts—at the time, they seemed so impressive.

Cries, moans, our important suffering.
A hand at the small of the back
or on the breast—

And now across the wall
someone is clearing the table,
wrapping the dark bread and the white ceramic pot of butter.

What did we think?
What did we talk about?

Upstairs, a light goes on.
It must be
Gwen's, it burns
the span of a story—

7.
Why love what you will lose?
There is nothing else to love.

8.
Last night in bed your
hand fell heavily upon
my shoulder. I thought

you slept. Yet we are
parted. Perhaps the sheet moved,
given your hand's weight by

the dampness of
my body. Morning: I have
written to thank you.

9.
The cat sleeps on the sidewalk,
black against the white cement.

The brave are patient.
They are the priests of sunrise,
lions on the ramparts, the promontory.

LEGEND

My father's father came
to New York from Dhlua:
one misfortune followed another.
In Hungary, a scholar, a man of property.
Then failure: an immigrant
rolling cigars in a cold basement.

He was like Joseph in Egypt.
At night, he walked the city;
spray of the harbor
turned to tears on his face.

Tears of grief for Dhlua—forty houses,
a few cows grazing the rich meadows—

Though the great soul is said to be
a star, a beacon,
what it resembles better is a diamond:
in the whole world there is nothing
hard enough to change it.

Unfortunate being, have you ceased to feel
the grandeur of the world
that, like a heavy weight, shaped
the soul of my grandfather?

From the factory, like sad birds his dreams
flew to Dhlua, grasping in their beaks
as from moist earth in which a man could see
the shape of his own footprint,
scattered images, loose bits of the village;
and as he packed the leaves, so within his soul

this weight compressed scraps of Dhlua
into principles, abstractions
worthy of the challenge of bondage:

in such a world, to scorn
privilege, to love
reason and justice, always
to speak the truth—

which has been
the salvation of our people
since to speak the truth gives
the illusion of freedom.

MORNING

The virtuous girl wakes in the arms of her husband,
the same arms in which, all summer, she moved
restlessly, under the pear trees:
it is pleasant to wake like this,
with the sun rising, to see the wedding dress
draped over the back of a chair,
and on the heavy bureau, a man's shirt, neatly folded;
to be restored by these
to a thousand images, to the church itself, the autumn sunlight
streaming through the colored windows, through
the figure of the Blessed Virgin, and underneath,
Amelia holding the fiery bridal flowers—
As for her mother's tears: ridiculous, and yet
mothers weep at their daughters' weddings,
everyone knows that, though
for whose youth one cannot say.
At the great feast there is always the outsider, the stranger to joy
and the point is how different they are, she and her mother.
Never has she been further from sadness
than she is now. She feels no call to weep,
but neither does she know
the meaning of that word, youth.

HORSE

What does the horse give you
that I cannot give you?

I watch you when you are alone,
when you ride into the field behind the dairy,
your hands buried in the mare's
dark mane.

Then I know what lies behind your silence:
scorn, hatred of me, of marriage. Still,
you want me to touch you; you cry out
as brides cry, but when I look at you I see
there are no children in your body.
Then what is there?

Nothing, I think. Only haste
to die before I die.

In a dream, I watched you ride the horse
over the dry fields and then
dismount: you two walked together;
in the dark, you had no shadows.
But I felt them coming toward me
since at night they go anywhere,
they are their own masters.

Look at me. You think I don't understand?
What is the animal
if not passage out of this life?